TABLE OF CONTENTS

Introduction

If you've recently been diagnosed as diabetic you must be feeling as if you're on a roller coaster. I remember vividly how discovering I had diabetes felt for me. If you've long battled sugar issues, then you've discovered that dealing with diabetes is more of a journey than a rapid ride.

I've written *The Diabetic Cookbook* for both newly diagnosed and long-time diabetics. Although I've included some favorite entrees and a week-long meal plan and suggestions about how to make beloved existing recipes diabetic friendly, this book is much more than a cookbook. I've tried to help those of you who are overwhelmed with questions of how to shop, what to prepare, how much to eat, and how to cook diabetic-friendly dishes that don't taste like sawdust. I know these were burning questions for me.

First, you need to know: Although you may be the only one in your circle of friends and relatives with diabetes, you are far from alone. In Canada, there are almost six million people with diabetic and prediabetic conditions—according to Diabetes Canada. The Centers for Disease Control put the figure for diabetes and prediabetes at more than a hundred million Americans.

Clearly, the large numbers of diagnosed and undiagnosed cases of diabetes is a cause for concern given the other related ailments that strike diabetics including: hypertension; higher incidence of heart and stroke; obesity; renal failure; blindness; foot and wound complications. Did you know that women with diabetes are twice as likely to have a heart attack? Obesity and diabetes have strong links. A family history of diabetes is also a warning factor.

The Diabetic Cookbook is not about symptoms of diabetes. It's not about tests to discover or monitor your glucose levels. Finally, *The Diabetic Cookbook* is not about the dangers of diabetes. These are all worthy topics. However, as the title suggests, *The Diabetic Cookbook* is all about ways to live with your diabetes diagnosis by changing how you shop, what you buy, what you eat, how much you eat, and when you eat. In short: the book is about healthy living with diabetes. I've even included a chapter on snacks!

A volume of literature discusses the importance of adopting a healthy lifestyle when you are living with diabetes. Healthline.com offers many common sense lifestyle changes. Many of them involve altering what we eat, when we eat, how much we eat. They also recommend in order to avoid peaks and spikes in blood sugar we eat smaller meals more often and keep to a strict schedule of when we eat. The Mayo Clinic guide to living with diabetes also suggests we eat carefully weighed portions and avoid overeating. Both Canadian and American Diabetes associations urge reading food labels hcarefully. I've devoted an entire chapter to how to read food labels and what to do with this information.

I'm not going to tell you living with diabetes is a piece of cake. Literally and figuratively it is NOT a piece of cake. Life with diabetes is much like becoming a parent: You will quickly discover it involves work every hour of every day, seven days a week with no vacations.

Much of *The Diabetic Cookbook* contains information about how to choose foods wisely and how to prepare them in order to regulate blood sugar. I've included important information that was shared with me during my diagnosis and other resources I've found helpful.

As with anything else, sharing information and resources is key to dealing with diabetes. Through your healthcare team and/or Internet links, get connected with others who are battling diabetes. Medical experts are invaluable but when it comes to those little questions that are niggling at you, having someone who empathizes and identifies is golden.

There's a common misunderstanding that, once you have diabetes, you must never eat anything containing sugar or carbs ever again. The good news is: You can still eat the foods you enjoy. The bad news is: You may have to limit the amount and/or the frequency of those foods.

When you meet with your healthcare team, they will calculate into your meal planning the foods you enjoy and ones you hate. There is some wiggle room.

Variety is a key to your meal plan as is when, what and how much you eat. Choose foods from vegetable, fruit, nuts, grains, and meats.

Chapter 1
Reading Food Labels

When you start eating food without labels, you no longer need to count calories.

What You'll Learn in this Chapter

- Why reading labels is vital to shopping and preparing food

- What's on a nutrition label

- How to interpret the label information

- How to find brands and products you trust

- Why keeping a food journal is key

- How to create and use your food journal data

Why Read Food Labels?

Let's face it! Reading food labels or nutrition labels is painstaking and a major time consumer. Why bother? When you pay attention to these labels, it allows you to compare various brands of the produce and find the one that best fits your nutritional requirements. For people with special dietary needs like diabetics, reading those food labels helps you limit things like sugars, carbs, fats. It also helps you ensure you are getting the recommended daily amounts of fiber, vitamins and protein.

In a perfect world, you'd buy only whole foods and cook everything you eat. That way, you'd ensure low-carb eating which is diabetic-friendly. But let's be realistic. Who has the time and who will realistically do this? That's why I've included a chapter on reading food labels and another on eating out.

What the Labels Tell You

When you read the nutrition label, it tells you the number of servings. This is important. So if the label says it contains five servings and that it contains 100 calories per serving then it is talking about 1/5 of the container—not the entire package.

The Mayo Clinic offers down-to-earth advice about the information contained on a food label and what to pay particular attention to if you are diabetic.

Food labels contain vital information such as the size of a serving; the number of calories per serving; total carbohydrates; % fiber; % salt; % sugar.

Begin by noting the ingredients. These are listed in order of most to least. Watch out for unhealthy ingredients like hydrogenated and partly hydrogenated oil as well as saturated fats. Avoid these foods. Look for such healthy ingredients as: soy, oats, whole wheat products and for monosaturated fats like olive oil, peanut butter, canola, and peanut oil.

Daily Value (DV) gives you information about how much nutrient there is in one serving. An easy rule of thumb for a diabetic is to choose foods which are lower DV fats and higher DV fiber.

Choose foods with less than 5% DV sodium. The foods that fit this category will be labeled "sodium free" or "salt free". Foods labeled "unsalted" or "no salt added" are not necessarily salt free. This label means simply no salt was added in the processing.

Other tips for diabetics: Aim for a minimum of 25 grams of fiber each day.

"Fat free" means less than ½ gram of fat per serving. "Low fat" means three grams or less per serving.

How Much?

The number of calories, fats, and carbs depends on the recommended amounts as determined by your dietitian. Before you shop, cook, and serve yourself, it's critical that you meet with a dietitian. He/she is trained to set the amounts so you control your blood sugar.

Note: This is a balancing act. How active you are; what your blood sugar is; your age; even your mental state affect what your body needs to keep your blood sugar stable.

In order to control your blood sugar with what you eat and your activity, you must balance what you eat, how much you consume, and when y0u eat. Your nutritional decisions are ones you and your dietitian, your diabetes consultant and perhaps your family doctor make as a healthcare team. Each of you possesses vital information for completing this task and maintaining that delicate balance.

Keeping a food journal is an excellent tool. It helps you know that you are eating right and it helps your healthcare team when it comes to making dietary changes to regulate your blood sugar. You can download a handy template, use an app, or use a checklist your nutrition team will give you. It is critical that you write down everything you eat and drink, the amount and the time you consumed it.

Good sources for food journal apps are:

Food Forecast:
http://www.diabetesforecast.org/2011/dec/keeping-a-food-journal.html

Fooducate:
https://www.healthline.com/health/diabetes/top-iphone-android-apps#Fooducate

A free app for both Apple and Android

A final thought: As the chapter quote suggests eating whole, non-processed foods negates the need for worrying about the ingredients. Bulk up your consumption of fresh fruits, vegetables, and whole grains for healthier living.

BEFORE WE CONTINUE

Thank you for reading so far, we hope you're finding this book informative. if you learn from this book and find it interesting, <u>please click here and leave a review</u>, I would be very grateful.

Chapter Two
Navigating the Grocery Store

Sometimes the wrong choices bring us to the right places.

What You'll Learn in this Chapter

- How to use your meal plan for weekly shopping
- How to prepare a weekly shopping list
- Where to buy most of your food items
- Smart shopping tips

One of the challenges in creating diabetic-friendly menus, meal plans, and dishes is shopping. When you are cooking for someone who has diabetes—whether it is for you or for a family member—your way of shopping changes. Many people have commented that cooking for a diabetic has improved the way the entire family eats.

A doctor has noted that if we all followed a diabetic diet we'd all be healthier.

Here are some shopping suggestions I've compiled from Diabetes Canada, dietitians and the Academy of Nutrition and Dietetics:

✓ Create a list based on your weekly meal plan. (I've included an example seven-day meal plan in a later chapter.) The most efficient way to do this is to create (or select) a meal plan for the week one day and then create a list of items you will need to purchase to take with you to the grocery store. If you have—for example—a monthly or four-week meal plan, you can create master grocery shopping lists for each week of that meal plan.

✓ Shop the outer walls of the grocery store. This is where you'll find fruit, vegetables, and whole foods, dairy, fish, chicken, that should constitute 70 or more percent of your diet. You may also choose to use farmers' markets or fruit stands for shopping these items.

✓ This is good advice for every shopper: Arrange your list so you are picking up items in each aisle as you go rather than crisscrossing the store back and forth.

✓ Another tip for all shoppers: Avoid—if at all possible—shopping on an empty stomach. This averts binge buying. For diabetics it's even more important. Research has shown that, when we're hungry, what we crave is high calorie items.

✓ Buy whole grain items. Just because an item says, "whole wheat" don't take it for granted. Read the food label. Look for whole grain listed first on the nutrition label. Learn which brands you can trust. For example Jill Weisenberger recommends: Mission Carb Balance soft taco tortillas; Pepperidge Farm Soft Honey Whole Wheat bread; Thomas' whole wheat bagel thins. If you stick with proven brands, shopping will be faster and more diabetic-friendly.

✓ When choosing canned fruits, vegetables, tuna, salmon select those with no salt added and things packed in water. Jill Weisenberger's picks include: Campbell's Butternut Squash soup; Eden Organic beans; Classico Tomato and Basil Sauce.

✓ "Sugar free" doesn't mean it's safe. The item might be high in carbs. Look at the nutrition label for grams of total carbohydrates.

✓ Choose seasonally available fruit and vegetables. When something is not available fresh, choose frozen. A good money saver is to buy in summer or fall when these items are inexpensive and freeze for use in winter and spring.

✓ Avoid anything containing trans fats!

✓ Stock up on healthy snack foods and prepackaged snack foods that are diabetic-friendly. Please see my chapter on "To Snack or not to Snack" for a list of healthy and non-healthy snack foods.

✓ When choosing meats, avoid processed, smoked, or cured meats. Select round roast, sirloin, pork tenderloin, and poultry free of hormones.

Chapter Three
Healthy Low-Carb Meal Plans

In my fantasy, low-carb doughnuts are possible.

Photo courtesy of stock photos

What You'll Learn in this Chapter

- The importance of a weekly or monthly meal plan

- Example seven-day meal plan

- Where to get additional meal plans

- How to create your own meal plans

Your healthcare team or your dietitian will suggest meal plans. But if you're like me, sometimes you get tired of the same old dishes. In this chapter, I've provided a seven-day meal plan that is diabetic- friendly. In the following chapters, I'll provide recipes for favorite low-carb entrée dishes you might like to prepare. They are ones I enjoy. They are also easy to prepare. I'm not a master chef and I don't enjoy long hours spent in the kitchen. However, I do need and want to eat well. So you're getting what works for me. I've included main lunch and dinner dishes. The rest of a five-meal daily meal plan pretty much looks after itself. See my chapter on meal plans to understand this.

I take little credit for this set of meal plans. I've derived them from my dietitian and from websites for Diabetes Canada and the American Diabetic Association. The mix and match part is mine. My goal is a maximum of 1200 calories spread over three meals and snacks.

I offer you these meal plans because, when I got started, I found it really hard to eat just 1200 calories and to spread these over the day in smaller, more frequent meals. Once I used this weekly meal plan for a month, I started to swap in my own dishes from the next chapter. By then, I'd gotten a feel for what amounts constituted my three meals and two snacks per day. Next, I graduated to creating my own meal plans. I shared these with my dietitian to make sure I was on the right track. She even duplicated my meal plans and recipes and shared them with others in her program. I was so proud.

You may be content to use this meal plan. You may even move on to swapping out items on this meal plan. You don't have to create your own meal plans ever. But it's something to consider down the road. The main advice I'd give you is: Proceed cautiously. Start with this meal plan—or one given to you by your dietitian. Move slowly to making changes.

Day One

Breakfast

A half-cup steel cut oaks cooked in water

1 plum chopped over oatmeal

4 walnut halves

Mid-morning Snack

Six ounces blueberries with ¼ cup plain yogurt

Lunch

Turkey Apple Melt

Use 2 slices whole-wheat bread. Slice half an apple over one slice of bread. Add 2 ounces of sliced, non-processed turkey. On the other slice of bread place 2 teaspoons of mustard, two tablespoons of shredded low fat cheese and a big handful of mixed greens. Put slices together. Toast in toaster oven until bubbly. Serve with extra greens.

Afternoon Snack

The other half of the apple from lunch. Add a pinch if cinnamon.

Dinner

Vegetable Soup One serving: 2 large cups vegetable soup. I make a vegetable soup ahead so I have some for one day and the rest for the next day's lunch. I start with low-fat, no-sodium chicken broth and add vegetables. You can be as inventive with the veggies as you wish.

Toast a slice of whole wheat bread and spread with a ½ cup goat cheese and a sprinkling of rosemary.

Day Two

Breakfast

Toast a bagel half. Cover with mashed avocado and serve with ½ cup blueberries and twenty-five pistachio nuts.

Mid-morning Snack

Ten cherries—I choose black but you can also have red cherries

Lunch

Remaining two cups of last night's vegetable soup along with a whole wheat baguette.

Afternoon Snack

Apple sliced. Add a pinch of cinnamon.

Dinner

Lentil Veggie Salad (Makes 3 ½ cups for dinner and 3 ½ cups for lunch on day three)

Cut up 4 cups broccoli

2 cups green beans

1 tablespoon olive oil

Pepper to taste

A ¾ cup green lentils

8 cups green lettuce

2 cups chopped kale

Chopped parsley tarragon, onion to taste.

Toss broccoli and green beans in olive oil. Add pepper to taste. Place on cookie sheet. Roast at 400 for 20 minutes.

While veggies are roasting, boil lentils in 2 ½ cups boiling water until tender (20 minutes) Rinse and drain.

Dressing: Mix a ½ cup low-fat mayonnaise, a ¼ c. low-fat buttermilk, a tablespoon or so squirt of lemon juice and herbs. You can be as liberal with herbs as you wish and/or you can add them to the salad. Process in food processor until smooth. (I often make this ahead.)

Toss lettuce and kale with roasted vegetables and lentils. Drizzle dressing over top or serve on the side. Save half for lunch on a later day. You'll find I cook several servings and freeze in single-serving packages for later meals.

For dessert? Half a banana and an ounce of dark chocolate

Day Three

Breakfast

6 ounces plain yogurt with a half- cup of berries. Add 1 tsp. ground flaxseed and 6 walnut halves.

Mid-morning Snack

A plum or an apricot

Lunch

The remaining 2 cups of the previous evening's soup with a toasted whole grain baguette.

Afternoon Snack

An orange

Dinner

<u>Chicken Sausage and Roasted Veggies, Rice and a Salad:</u>

Use a cup and a half of this recipe and save the rest for a future meal.

Add a half-cup of (cooked) brown rice. Add Italian salt-free seasoning and oregano to taste.

Cut yellow and/or orange and/or red peppers in strips

Create onion circles

Chop veggies of choice

Place 12 ounces of chicken sausage (I use Italian flavored) on cookie sheet in 425 degree oven. Roast 10-15 minutes. Then add veggies, peppers, onions and roast until tender stirring to avoid sticking. Add Italian seasoning and oregano to taste.

Serve with brown rice. Add a salad made with a cup and a half greens, ¼ cup shredded carrot, ¼ cup sliced cucumbers and vinaigrette dressing on the side.

Day Four

Breakfast

A half-cup of steel-cut oatmeal cooked in 1 cup water. Add 2 tsp. ground flax seed and top with a plum and one and a half chopped walnuts.

Mid-morning Snack

Ten cherries—I choose black but you can also have red cherries

Lunch

Veggie Hummus Sandwich

On two slices of whole wheat bread spread 3 tablespoons of hummus. Add a ¼ mashed avocado, a ¼ sliced red pepper, a ¼ cup sliced cucumber, a ¼ cup shredded carrot, and a ½ cup greens.

Make ahead if you wish. I usually make two or three and wrap in foil for later lunches. I nuke it before eating but you could put it in the toaster oven or serve cold.

Finish off with three apricots

Afternoon Snack

One apple, sliced. Add a pinch of cinnamon.

Dinner

Salmon (This makes four servings. You can save the extra three for future meals or invite friends!)

Add 2 cups of water to 2/3 cup farro. Bring to a boil. Reduce heat and simmer until tender (1/2 hr.

Chop an eggplant into 1" cubes and a red pepper into strips. Cut a squash into 1" cubes. Add a cup and a half of cherry tomatoes. Cut an onion into rings. Toss veggies in 3 T. olive oil. Place on foil lined cookie sheet in 450 degree oven. Roast 30 minutes or until tender stirring to avoid sticking.

Season a pound of wild salmon with lemon zest, pepper and no-salt Italian seasoning to taste. Cut into four pieces. Roast on foil-lined pan on lower rack for six to ten minutes. Drizzle with 2 tsp. honey and red-wine vinegar to taste.

Serve salmon, veggies and farro with lemon wedges. This is four servings. Wrap 3 servings and save for future meals.

Day Five

Breakfast

Toast a bagel half. Cover with mashed avocado and serve with ½ cup blueberries and twenty-five pistachio nuts.

Mid-morning Snack

Six dried apricots.

Lunch

Turkey-Fruit Melt

Stuff a pita pocket with three to four ounces of low-salt turkey slices. Slice half a pear or apple and add. Sprinkle with low-fat cheese and toast in toaster oven. Serve with a cup of mixed greens.

Finish lunch with a plum or an apricot.

Afternoon Snack

Slice the other half of the apple or pear from lunch. Add a pinch of cinnamon.

Dinner

Meatballs with Spaghetti Squash

Cut a three-to-four-pound spaghetti squash in half. Remove seeds. Bake face down in the oven at 325 until squash is tender. Scoop the squash out of the two baked shell halves. Place squash in a fry pan with 2 T. olive oil. Brown 10 minutes. Add a half a cup chopped parsley, a quarter of a cup low-fat Parmesan cheese and 1 T no-salt Italian seasoning.

Place a pound of turkey meatballs in 1 T. olive oil in large skillet. Cook over medium heat 6 to 8 minutes. Meatballs should be brown.

To the skillet, add a large can of low-sodium crushed tomatoes, onion powder and chopped oregano. Stir until sauce simmers.

Serve over spaghetti squash. Sprinkle with ¼ cup Parmesan cheese. Add a cup of salad greens and a toasted whole wheat bagel round.

Day Six

Breakfast

A four-ounce serving plain yogurt, 2 ½ crushed walnuts, 1 tsp ground flaxseed.

Mid-morning Snack

Fourteen grapes

Lunch

Two and a half cups of homemade vegetable soup (from previous recipe) and a whole wheat baguette.

Afternoon Snack

An apple, sliced. Add a pinch of cinnamon.

Dinner

Chicken Breast with Squash

Half a cup of baked butternut squash (Cook the whole quash. Save the rest for future meals.)

Spinach salad with red onion, half an apple, sliced, and ten mandarin orange slices

Broil two four-ounce chicken breasts in 350 degree oven until chicken is tender (40 minutes).

Glaze with no-sugar-added apple jelly, shredded lemon zest and ½ tsp. ginger.

This chicken dish makes two servings. Share or wrap one for later dinner.

Day Seven

Breakfast

Toast a blueberry bagel half. Top with 3 T. frozen or fresh blueberries and 2 tsp. ground flaxseed.

Mid-morning Snack

An orange

Lunch

Half a whole wheat pita round smeared with a quarter cup hummus.

2 cups salad greens, ½ c. sliced cucumber, and ¼ c. shredded carrot. Vinaigrette dressing on the side.

Afternoon Snack

An apple, sliced. Add a pinch of cinnamon.

Dinner

Pork Chops with Brussel Sprouts and Rice

Steam Brussel sprouts with sun-dried tomato pesto

Place half a cup of uncooked brown rice in 2 cups water. Add a half-cup of mixed frozen vegetables as rice is cooking. I cook my rice in a casserole in the oven but you can do it in a saucepan or in the microwave. I bake the chops in a roast pan in the oven at the same time.

Cook four boneless loin chops in a large skillet in 1T. olive oil. Drain.

Add 2 cups of sliced onion, a 6 ounce can of low-fat low-sodium mushroom soup, one diced apple, Worcestershire sauce, dried thyme, and garlic powder to taste. Add half a pound of sliced mushrooms. Place in crock pot or roast pan in oven. I roast mine in the oven while the rice is also cooking there.

Cook 8 hours on low or 4 hours on high or an hour in 325 degree oven.

Garnish with rosemary or parsley sprigs.

Chapter Four
Low-Carb Dishes

I don't always serve "potatoes" in my low-carb kitchen. When I do, it's most often riced cauliflower or radishes.

What You'll Learn in this Chapter

- How to prepare low-carb diabetic-friendly entrees

- Tasty dishes that can be included as lunch or dinner items in your meal plan

- Amounts that constitute single servings of each dish

If, when you read the title of this book, you expected a recipe book, then chapters three and four are going to be of special interest to you.

Why is this book not a chapter-by-chapter collection of diabetic-friendly recipes? That's simple! When I was first diagnosed, reading and collecting recipes was the farthest thing from my mind. I wanted to know: what I could eat; when and how often I should eat; how much I could consume. The recipe adventure came much later after I learned to follow a meal plan, how to shop for that plan, and how to prepare those simple recipes I've included in that meal plan.

When it comes to recipes, there is nothing new under the sun—or in the oven. I am not a chef. But I am a good researcher. The recipes I am including are the result of my dietitian's ingenuity and my combing websites to find things I like and ingredients that are diabetic-friendly. Most of the ones I've included are entrees or lunch dishes. You see: I don't find it difficult to find snacks, salads, vegetable dishes. On the rare occurrence I crave something sweet I limit myself to a bite. But entrees and what constitutes one serving are puzzling to me. Hence I am sharing entrée ideas.

Here are some of my favorites. I encourage you to try them and to do your own research to find others that appeal to you. Remember: We are our own best resource. Talk to your healthcare team. Join a chat room for diabetics. Share your knowledge and gain from others' trial and error.

Beet Soup

(Serves 8)

1 tsp. olive oil

A chopped red onion

4 cups of chicken broth (I make my own but you can buy no-salt, low-fat broth)

2 cups of water

4 beets cooked, peeled, chopped

1 potato cooked, peeled chopped

1 t. lemon juice

Half a cup of low-fat sour cream

Sauté onion. Add beets, potato water and broth. Simmer. Puree in food processor or with hand puree appliance. Divide soup into eight portions. (I keep extra for later lunches). Serve with a swirl of sour cream.

Ginger Pumpkin Bisque

(Serves 6)

In a crock pot, put a large (14 ounce) can of pumpkin. Add a diced pear, 1 ½ cups of diced onion and a pint (16 ounces) of low-salt, low-fat chicken broth. Add pepper, cumin, nutmeg and ginger to taste. Cook on high 4 hours or on low 7 hours.

Puree the mixture and add 2 cups of coconut milk OR evaporated skim milk and a quarter of a cup of unsweetened applesauce. Mix in 1 ½ T. Splenda. Simmer 30 minutes.

Before serving add a dollop of fat-free plain yogurt to the bowl.

Grilled Pork and Homemade Salsa

(Serves 6)

Salsa:

Combine a can of crushed (packed in its own juice) pineapple with a chopped orange and 2 T. chopped cilantro.

Pork:

Make a rub of ½ T. brown sugar; 2 T. minced garlic; 2 tsp minced ginger; 2 tsp. each of coriander and cumin; ½ tsp. turmeric. Add 2 T. olive oil.

Rub this on 6 pork loin chops—both sides.

BBQ on medium high for 5 minutes each side. Serve with salsa, roasted veggies, and brown rice.

Chicken for Four

Place four four-ounce skinless chicken breasts in a bag with 1 T olive oil. Sprinkle on rosemary, minced garlic, and pepper to taste. Add a quarter of a cup of dry red wine and 3 T. balsamic vinegar. Refrigerate overnight.

Place coated chicken in a shallow cooking dish in 450 degree oven and bake 10 to 15 minutes or until meat thermometer reads 170 F. Serve with roasted veggies and a salad.

Diabetic-Friendly Burgers

(Makes 4 servings)

Drain 2 cups of chick peas. Add a quarter of a cup of diced onion or chives and a quarter cup of chopped parsley or coriander, a quarter of a cup of shredded carrots, and a quarter of a cup of bran cereal crumbs. Add 3 T. lemon juice, 3T. water, and 2 T. ground sesame seeds. Add minced garlic and pepper to taste. Place in food processor and pulse until chick peas are smooth. Mix and form into 4 patties.

Heat 2 t. olive oil in a Teflon skillet. Cook on medium for four-five minutes or until golden, flipping patties halfway through.

Serve with this sauce. (I make it ahead)

A quarter of a cup of no-fat sour cream, 2 T. ground sesame seeds, 2 T. chopped parsley, 2 T. water, and 2 t. lemon juice. Add pepper and minced garlic to taste. Whisk and refrigerate until needed.

Baked Rainbow Trout

(Makes 2 servings)

Cut a one-pound trout into 2 medium fillets, split lengthwise. Place trout fillets in a sprayed shallow baking dish.

Mix a half-cup of parsley or coriander, ½ t. grated lime zest, 2 T. lime juice, and 1 t. olive oil. Add pepper to taste. Add 2 cups of chopped tomato. Set aside to marinate.

Bake fish in a 400-degree oven until the fish is flaky. Lift thee tomatoes out of marinate and serve to the side of the trout fillets. Drizzle the remaining marinade over the fish.

Lamb Stew

(Makes 4 servings)

Cut a pound of lean boneless lamb into 1" pieces. Brown the lamb cutes in a skillet with 1 T, of olive oil. Set aside. In the skillet, add 3 T. of olive oil, one large chopped onion, 4 cloves of minced garlic, 1 T. of oregano and half a teaspoon of hot pepper flakes. Cook five minutes.

In a large soup pot or roast pan, place the meat and onion mixture. Add a large can (14 ounces) of diced tomatoes— juice and all, 3 cups of frozen or canned lima beans, a red and a green pepper chopped, and a cup homemade chicken broth (You can use no salt, low-fat packaged broth). Add pepper and fresh parsley to taste. Bake in the roast pan or simmer on the stove top in the soup pot for 40 minutes.

Mango Chicken

(Makes 6 servings)

In a large zip lock bag combine: 2 T. of ground tapioca, 1 T. of paprika, a 1/2 T. of nutmeg, a ½ T of cloves, and a pinch of red chili flakes. Add four boneless skinless chicken breasts. Shake the chicken to coat it.

Place the chicken in a flat casserole dish. Drizzle it with 2 T of olive oil. Bake in 350 F oven until the chicken is browned. Add a half-cup of minced red onion, a 14-ounce can of coconut milk, a 14-ounce can of diced unsalted tomatoes, and a cup of mango chunks (frozen or canned is fine). Cook for 30 minutes.

Serve the chicken with steamed brown rice. (I cook the rice in the oven in a casserole while the chicken is baking.)

Grilled One-Dish Dinner

(Makes 12 servings)

In a deep skillet or a Dutch oven put 2 T. of olive oil. Add one inch cubes of squash, eggplant and carrot. When these are tender add four sliced red peppers, 3 cups of red onion slices, broccoli and cauliflower florets. Cook these vegetables over medium heat until they are soft enough to eat (18-20 minutes). Add any cubed meat of your choice—turkey, chicken, ham, or beef… Stir and cook the dish until meat is hot. I package the rest of the dish into eleven individual size portions and freeze or refrigerate them for later.

Serve with brown rice and a salad.

Coconut Shrimp

(Makes 4 servings.)

Thaw a pound of large shrimp or use fresh jumbo shrimp.

Beat a quarter cup of Egg Beaters or two egg whites.

Grind a cup of bran cereal or steel cut oats. Add 1/3 of a cup of shredded unsweetened coconut and a pinch of ginger and pepper to taste. Stir crumb mixture.

Dip the shrimp in the egg mixture and then roll it in crumbs. Place the coated shrimp on a foil-lined cookie sheet. Bake the shrimp at 325 F for 8-10 minutes or until it is lightly browned.

Cook half a pound of brown and/or long grain rice in a pot or in the microwave in 2 cups of water. I place the rice in a casserole in oven with 2 cups of water and cook it while I am baking the shrimp. When rice is soft, add a half-cup of fresh, frozen, or canned chopped mango, a half-cup of diced green onion or chives and 2 T. of cilantro to the rice.

Place the baked shrimp over a bed of rice and sprinkle it with chopped cilantro.

Slow Cooker Beef Stew

Cut beef into 1" cubes and place them in a crock pot. Add 2 sweet potatoes cut in 1" cubes, 2 cups of frozen green beans, and one onion, cut into rings. Add a jar of low-salt chunk salsa. Stir in a (14 ounces) can of low-salt beef broth. Add 1 t. of basil and 2 cloves of minced garlic. Cover the stew and cook it on low for 8-1o hours or on high for 4 hours.

Put stew in soup bowls. Just before serving, sprinkle each soup bowl of stew with low-fat Pepper Jack cheese.

Enchiladas

(Makes 12 servings)

Set the oven at 350° F. In a large skillet, put 2 cloves of minced garlic, and a quarter cup of low-salt chicken broth. Cook on medium for a minute. Add a half-cup of green chilies, and a minced onion. Stir for 3 minutes. Add 3 cups of cooked chicken or turkey. Heat until meat is warm.

Coat an oblong 9"-by-13"pan. Divide the chicken mixture among 12 whole wheat tortillas. Place the mixture at one end of one tortilla. Roll up. Place seam side down in dish. Do this with all twelve tortillas. Top the tortillas with low-salt salsa or enchilada sauce. Sprinkle the tortillas with two cups (8 oz.) of low-fat Pepper Jack cheese. Bake for 2o minutes or until the dish is bubbly.

Avocado BLT

(Serves 4)

Mash an avocado. Add 2 T. of lemon juice.

Spread this mixture on eight slices of whole wheat toast. Top with a quarter-cup of cilantro, tomato slices, turkey bacon and salad greens.

Put two slices together to form four sandwiches. Toast them in a toaster oven. Or, sprinkle each open-faced slice of bread slice and avocado topping with low fat cheese. Toast them in a toaster oven and serve them open-faced, adding salad greens on the side.

Tandoori Turkey

(Serves 4)

First make the chutney and set it aside:

Peel and chop one pear. Quarter or chop a cup of fresh or frozen cherries. Chop and add a small red pepper and a quarter-cup of mango chutney. Stir in an eighth of a cup of chopped red onion. Add a T. of lime juice.

In a bowl, mix 1 t. of curry powder, 1 t. of paprika, and 1 t. of cumin. Coat both sides of 4 turkey cutlets with mixture.

Heat a skillet on medium. Cook turkey for two minutes per side or until it is no longer pink. Serve the turkey with the chutney and a salad.

Japanese Chicken and Noodles

(Makes 6 servings)

In a large fry pan, mix a ½ t. of sesame oil, 1 T. of canola oil and 2 T. of chili paste. Stir. Add 2 cloves of minced garlic. Stir. Add 4 chicken breasts cut into 1" cubes and ¼ c. low sodium soya sauce. Fry until chicken is not pink (5 minutes). (I often use leftover cooked chicken instead.) Place the chicken mixture on a warm plate.

Cook and drain half a pound of soba noodles.

To the liquid in the pan add half a head of cabbage, shredded and 2 shredded carrots. Stir fry the mixture for two minutes. Add the cooked drained noodles. Stir. Add the chicken mixture. Stir and serve.

Baked Red Snapper

(Serves 4)

In a skillet, put 2 T. of olive oil and a thinly sliced onion. Sauté until soft (20 minutes).

Preheat the oven to 400 degrees. Place a pound of red snapper fillets, cut lengthwise, in a shallow baking dish. Add ¼ c. of lemon juice, 1 T. of olive oil and 2 t. of balsamic vinegar. Spoon sautéed onions over fish.

Bake 20 minutes or until fish is flaky.

Serve the fish with a salad and steamed veggies.

I use this recipe for salmon, catfish and whitefish too.

Taco in a Bowl

(Serves 4)

In 1 t. of olive oil, brown a pound of lean ground turkey.

Assemble the following ingredients in four bowls dividing the mixture evenly among the bowls. Start with the lettuce:

4 cups of torn romaine or other type of lettuce

A 1/2 cup of low-sodium salsa

A 2 c. of minced red onions

A 1/2 c. of chopped cilantro

1 can or 4 oz. sliced olives (I use black but you can use green.) 4 lime wedges

Sprinkle ground beef over top. Add a dollop of no-fat sour cream and sprinkle with shredded Pepper Jack cheese. Top with 4 ounces kettle baked crumbled corn tortilla chips

Chapter Five:
Adapting Favorite Recipes

As the Pillsbury Dough Boy said, "Nothin' says lovin' like something from the oven!" One of my greatest regrets in cooking diabetic-friendly foods was giving up dishes I treasured. Here are ways to adapt old favorites.

What You'll Learn in this Chapter

- How to adapt favorite dishes to make them diabetic-friendly

- How you can still enjoy those "sinful" dishes

- "Trades" you can make in baking favorite dishes so they're diabetic-friendly

You need not throw out the recipes that you loved before diabetes. You can make some simple adaptations that allow you to have things you've enjoyed without violating diabetic-friendly eating. Here are some tricks I've learned from clever dietitians:

✓ Trade butter or margarine for unsweetened applesauce in recipes.

✓ Use a sugar-free cake mix to create diabetic-legal brownies or trifle.

✓ Use sugar-free ice cream for a "decadent" diabetic-legal dessert.

✓ Cut sugar in half for many dishes.

- ✓ Use cinnamon, nutmeg, garlic, and other herbs and spices to enhance the taste and make things taste "sweeter" or "tastier".

- ✓ Substitute Splenda cup for cup for sugar.

- ✓ Serve quick breads instead of cake or cookies

- ✓ Spray pans and cookie sheets instead of using butter or margarine.

- ✓ Instead of fats, use vegetable oils like olive or canola oil. For example: Use 2/3 cup vegetable oil for a cup of butter or margarine.

- ✓ Substitute egg whites for whole eggs. 2 egg whites= one egg

- ✓ Substitute lean meats like ground turkey for beef.

- ✓ Remove skin from poultry and visible fat from meats.

- ✓ Reduce fat in recipes by one third.

- ✓ Substitute skim milk or water for whole milk.

- ✓ Use evaporated skim milk for cream.

- ✓ Chill soups, gravies, chili. Skim off hardened fat and then reheat.

- ✓ Use low fat crackers, cheeses, skim milk, low fat cottage cheese, non-fat yogurt, low-fat soups.

- ✓ Use low-fat mayonnaise and margarine.

- ✓ Cut salt from recipes. Substitute seasonings like garlic and ginger instead.

- ✓ Add fiber by using ½ whole wheat flour in recipes.

- ✓ Grind bran cereals and use for ¼ of flour in recipes.

- ✓ Use brown rice and/or wild rice instead of white rice.
- ✓ Use oatmeal for half of meat in meatloaf and chili.
- ✓ Add beans and reduce meat in chili and meatloaf.
- ✓ Add raisins, apples, blueberries to cookies, breads instead of chocolate chips.
- ✓ Serve raw veggies and salad greens with meals.

Chapter Six
To Snack or not to Snack

Poster courtesy of Green Tidings.com

What You'll Learn in this Chapter

- Why snacking is an important topic for diabetics

- How to select "prepackaged" snacks that are diabetic-friendly

- How to avoid mid-afternoon binge eating at the vending machine

- How to create your own diabetic-friendly snacks

You're probably wondering: Why include a chapter on snacking in what is primarily a low-carb cookbook? Well here's why: Snacks are considered an important component of many—not all—diabetic meal plans. So, knowing how to select ready-made snacks and—better yet—create in-house snacks becomes an important part of a diabetic food plan.

The jury is still out on the value of snacking. Not every dietitian recommends snacking. Not every diabetic require snacks. Basically, snacking—for a diabetic—means dividing your total daily food intake into three meals with one, two, or three snacks in between meals. Snacking isn't always crucial for diabetics. That said: snacks may be vital for the meal plan of some diabetics.

If you are someone who needs—or prefers—to include snacks in your eating plan, there are some important rules. Snacks are not an add-on. They are part of the total calories suggested by your dietitian. Snacks are a way to spread your food consumption more evenly over twenty-four hours than breakfast, lunch, and dinner would be.

It should go without saying—but I'll say it anyway: Your snacks should be healthy. This means, unfortunately, that the snacks in the "snack aisle" of your grocery store are almost all verboten. The so-called snack aisle is full of unhealthy sugars and carbs. These often-empty calories are what contribute to weight gain, obesity—and yes—diabetes.

Where can you find healthy snack choices? In the outside walls of your supermarket or at the farmers' market.

You might also consider those hundred-calorie choices. These help reduce calories for a quick between-meal pick-me-up. Better yet! Create your own hundred-calorie portions. Simply make smaller packages from larger ones. It's more economical and takes little time.

Diabetic-Friendly Ready-Made Snacks

- ✓ Low-fat, whole-grain crackers. Look for ones with two or more grams of fiber per serving
- ✓ Avoid any trans-fat snacks
- ✓ Choose snacks with 15 grams—or less— carbohydrates.
- ✓ Combine crackers with protein like peanut butter, hummus, low-fat cheese, tuna, or hard-boiled egg
- ✓ Nuts are an excellent snack—eaten in small portions. Choose unsalted almonds, walnuts, or mixed nuts
- ✓ Sun Chips Harvest Cheddar (100-calorie pack)
- ✓ Orville Redenbacher's Smart Pop popcorn (3 ½ cups popped)
- ✓ Quaker Snack Mix Baked Cheddar
- ✓ Star Kissed Solid Albacore Tuna (in water)
- ✓ Planter's Dark Chocolate Forest Blend trail mix
- ✓ Sun Maid Mediterranean dried apricots
- ✓ Triscuit Thin Crisp crackers
- ✓ Del Monte Fruit Natural Snack Packs (no sugar added)
- ✓ Nature Valley Oats and Honey crunchy granola snack bars
- ✓ Kettle Baked Potato Chips
- ✓ True North Peanut Clusters

✓ Genisoy Soy Cheddar Cheese Crisps

Snacks to Avoid

✓ Any snacks containing trans fats. Chips or pretzels in reduced fat and low salt can occasionally be a good snack.

✓ Granola bars and cookies—even when they sound healthy have high sugar and low fiber. Read labels carefully or make your own.

✓ If you crave something—like chocolate or a cookie—choose a bite and enjoy very infrequently.

✓ Sugary cereals

✓ Maple, agave, honey and any sugary sauces

✓ Dried fruit

✓ Sugar-sweetened beverages—including juices

✓ Fruit-flavored yogurt

✓ Frozen yogurt and ice cream

✓ French fries

Make Your Own Healthy Snacks

Make these up ahead in single portions and grab for a snack on the run or to take to work with you. These healthy snacks avoid that run to the vending machine where NOTHING is good for you!

✓ Guacamole—I make my own but you can buy diabetic-friendly ones by reading labels

✓ Unsalted nuts

✓ Strawberries and blueberries

- ✓ Hummus—I make my own but you can buy diabetic-friendly ones by reading labels
- ✓ Roasted unsalted seeds
- ✓ Unsalted popcorn
- ✓ Greek yogurt
- ✓ Peanut and almond butter
- ✓ Raw vegetables—especially broccoli and cauliflower but you can mix and match.
- ✓ Cheese rounds or cheese sticks
- ✓ Apple slices
- ✓ Roasted almonds
- ✓ Tuna or salmon packed in water

Chapter Eight
Eating Out

Never accept limitations!
~Jack Byrne

What You'll Learn in this Chapter

- How to make eating out fit your schedule

- How to select menu items that are diabetic-friendly

- How to limit portion size so it fits your caloric requirements

Granted, it's much harder to control what you eat, how much you consume and when you eat if you travel and/or eat out. However, it is possible. Diabetes Canada offers these common sense tips:

✓ Sticking to a strict schedule is vital to maintaining blood sugar levels. Choose a restaurant that takes reservations and book a time that fits your meal plan. If others will be dining with you, simply explain why the time is important.

✓ Don't hesitate to ask about how the food is prepared. Ask for a dish without the sauce, a salad with oil and vinegar on the side and dishes prepared without salt or butter and broiled or poached—never fried or breaded. If side dishes are high in carbs ask for extra steamed vegetables instead. Most restaurants are very accommodating but you need to ask!

✓ Good choices? Fatty fish like salmon prepared by broiling or poaching; spinach salad with grilled chicken breast; grilled skinless chicken with veggies and a salad. Try to eat out like you would at home. Ask for your entree baked, poached, broiled, or grilled—never fried!

✓ Avoid large portions. You know by now what consitutes a "legal" portion. Ask for a ½ portion or take half home for tomorrow. Eat slowly so you are not tempted to finish that whole portion! You can even ask the waiter to bring a box with your meal so you can box half before you eat and avoid temptation.

✓ Avoid sugared beverages—even juice. Choose water or herbal tea or unsweetened or artifically sweetened drinks. If you have a glass of wine, those calories must be counted as part of your intake. It's often easier and safer to stick to non-alcoholic, unsweetened drinks!

✓ Watch out for dressings and sauces. They'red often loaded with sugar. Ask for sauceless dishes. Choose oil and vinegar dressings or bring your own diabetic-friendly dressing.

✓ Beware of those appetizers. They count. Either avoid them altogether or count them as part of your meal's calories. Avoid that tantalizing bread that lands on your table before entrees.

It's possible to eat out at a friend's house or go to a restaurant but you have to exert self control in these situations and eat wisely! Seek restaurants that cater to your needs. Do not hesitate to suggest these places when friends suggest dining out. When entertaining friends serve what you can and do eat. If friends consult you about the menu they intend to serve, be helpful and informative. You might even offer to bring a diabetic-friendly dessert.

Conclusion

Whether you're a newly diagnosed diabetic or you've been struggling with this challenge for years, I hope *The Diabetic Cookbook* will be a useful tool in your fight. I've provided recipes that were shared with me as well as some new ones I've developed since I encountered "sugar issues". As well, I've attached some resources that have been particularly helpful.

As we continue our journey in finding a healthy lifestyle, sharing what works for each of us is vital. While our symptoms may vary, there are many common elements and ways to live healthy with diabetes.

You need not think that being diabetic is a death sentence. Research has shown that making nutritionally sound changes to your diet, moving your body vigorously for at least thirty minutes a day and checking sugar levels carefully can significantly improve your health. In some cases it can even prevent getting type 2 diabetes.

Knowledge is power. The more you know about diabetes and how to live well with it the healthier and happier you will be. I hope The Diabetic Cookbook becomes a well-used handbook for you.

Resources

Bowers, E. "9 Diabetes-Friendly Grocery Shopping Tips". https://www.everydayhealth.com/hs/type-2-diabetes-live-better-guide/grocery-shopping-tips/

Diabetes Canada. "Understanding Nutrition Labels". https://www.diabetes.ca/diabetes-and-you/healthy-living-resources/diet-nutrition/understanding-the-nutrition-label

Diabetes Care Community. "Welcome to Self-Management Resources". https://www.diabetescarecommunity.ca/self-management-resources/

Health.com. "20 Tasty Diabetic-Friendly Recipes". http://www.health.com/health/gallery/0,,20307365,00.html

Heathline.com. "Type 2 Diabetes Diet Recommendations". https://www.healthline.com/health/type-2-diabetes#diet-recommendations

Healthline.com. "Managing Type 2 Diabetes". https://www.healthline.com/health/type-2-diabetes#managing-type-diabetes

LaBarbera, M. "Reading Food Labels: How Does it Help Buy Healthier Foods?". http://www.nourishinteractive.com/healthy-living/free-nutrition-articles/161-family-facts-importance-reading-food-labels

Mayo Clinic. "Reading Food Labels: Tips if You Have Diabetes". https://www.mayoclinic.org/diseases-conditions/diabetes/in-depth/food-labels/art-20047648

McCulloch, M. and Marsden, L. "Top 25 Diabetic Snacks" in *Diabetic Living*.
http://www.diabeticlivingonline.com/food-to-eat/nutrition/top-25-diabetic-snacks

National Institute of Diabetes and Digestive and Kidney Diseases. "Diabetes Diet, Eating and Healthy Activity".
https://www.niddk.nih.gov/health-information/diabetes/overview/diet-eating-physical-activity

Neithercot, T. "Keeping a Food Journal".
http://www.diabetesforecast.org/2011/dec/keeping-a-food-journal.html

Theobald, M. "8 Tips for Eating out with Diabetes".
https://www.everydayhealth.com/type-2-diabetes/diet/eating-out-with-diabetes/

Weisenberger, J. "Quick Guide to Grocery Shopping for Diabetics" in *Diabetic Living*.
http://www.diabeticlivingonline.com/food-to-eat/nutrition/quick-guide-to-grocery-shopping-diabetes

Made in the USA
Monee, IL
18 June 2021